Keeping Time with
Blue Hyacinths

Keeping Time with Blue Hyacinths

Sholeh Wolpé

The University of Arkansas Press
Fayetteville • 2013

Copyright © 2013 by Sholeh Wolpé

ISBN-10: 1-55728-628-0
ISBN-13: 978-1-55728-628-4

17 16 15 14 13   5 4 3 2 1

Text design by Ellen Beeler

♾ The paper used in this publication meets the minimum requirements of
the American National Standard for Permanence of Paper for Printed Library
Materials Z39.48-1984.

Library of Congress Cataloging-in-Publication Data

Wolpé, Sholeh.
    [Poems. Selections]
    Keeping time with blue hyacinths / Sholeh Wolpé.
        pages cm
    Includes bibliographical references.
    Poems.
    "Includes the meditation 'Keeping Time with Blue Hyacinths: A Nowruz
Sonata in Seven Movements.'"
    ISBN 978-1-55728-628-4 (paperback : alk. paper)
    ISBN 1-55728-628-0 (paperback : alk. paper)
    I. Title.
    PK6449.E5K44 2013
    811'.6—dc23

                                                                    2012041984

For
Nathalie, Suzanne, and Tony
my three steady lamps

Contents

"Whenever you find yourself on the side of the majority, it is time to reform."

Keeping Time with Blue Hyacinths

"the best way out is
always through"

—Robert Frost

Ash

To put a cigarette between her fingers, just so,
bring it to her lips and inhale, just so,
launch smoke rings in the air, just so.
What could be *cooler* than that?

Then, she dips her finger in ash
and draws
clouds beneath her feet,
a bridge of hearts to a big house,
a tall spectacled spouse, a German Shepherd,
awards, diplomas, and pictures
of love under sheets soft as moss,
of rainy Sunday mornings with pancakes,
children barely out of dreams, sweet
hot butter dripping from their mouths,
New Year's pajama parties with friends,
a secret herb garden behind a rusty door.

Beneath this blizzard of ash a husband
examining her head with a stethoscope,
declares her absurd. Her son lives and dies,
dies and lives again,
a gun smokes against a beloved forehead
and the willow in the yard weeps sap.

In her homeland a bird's egg hatches a wolf,
her childhood house coughs black smoke,
and roads turn to dead-end alleys.

Then, she draws a lover, pours her dark
curls like tar into his hands,
feeds word fed to a locomotive
bound for a place called *away*,
and tells herself: this is exile.

In the end, her face a map of ashen roads,
she goes to the sink, lathers and rubs,
slowly raises her chin to the mirror.

The Chill

On the bed's edge,
that precipice of loneliness,
sleep withholds its grace.

He presses his groin to her ass,
his warm hands loving her breasts,
the hollow of her waist,
her shoulder's arching bones,

kisses the nape of her neck,
sinks his head in her hair like a man
who's seen the dark ghosts of fog.

She wants to trample
this pain, give him
the lions in her throat,
the swans in her groin,
these wolves in her hips,

but her skin cries no, her bones
won't budge, and her tongue refuses.

When he pulls away, cold air stirs,
awakens a chill that freezes
and rends their lives into
a thousand irretrievable shards.

The Honeymoon Cruise

As they watch the sun water-ski
on the horizon in a splash of red,
he says his friend warned him this is how
he would feel in the beginning.

Suffocated, cramped, and cornered
are words that can grease
a runway into the sea.

Later that night she stands alone
on the topmost deck. The wind wrestles
her hair, and she thinks, *Yes, it's that easy.*

He apologizes later that night.
A passing thing, he says.
A reed that bends to other men's breath, she says.
This is how the story continues.

Matrimony

The sheer curtain she hangs between
two open windows becomes
the tongue of the wind—
a dialogue between landscapes.

But the windows close,
and the curtain falls
into an unbreakable hush.

Each day

she wakes up and something's changed.
The parrot in the cage has stopped speaking English.
The line of ants has skipped the syrup.
The lawn has changed its mind
and is now leaning left.

The radio has gone opera, and the bananas
have softened for the strawberries.
The air, sabotaged by light, now courses
from the china cabinet towards the knife
drawer, and the skylights leaks leaves.

The crows have dipped their tails in white paint,
the fat pygmy goat is in love with a coyote,
and love has become so red, the trees have bent
their leafy heads, coughing blood.

Measure

Some things mildew too quickly
away from the sun.

He has a neck pain, she sees ghosts,
he wears a lead belt, she builds wings.
He says stick to the facts,
she says the sheets smell of longing.

What's buried among their bed's decaying springs?

He says I love you, she says I love you
to something she cannot see in the dark.

Affairs

The wrong way on the autobahn.
How many moths to a windshield?

How many men to one woman?
One man to raise iron walls;

two to turn a garden upside down;
three to shell a home, the children inside;

four to throw kerosene on a heart;
five to steal poems from the eyes.

The moths splatter on the glass,
winged question marks.

Vision

She picks up her husband's glasses,
puts them on the bridge of her nose,
looks in the bedroom mirror.

The thick lenses see two wives
—blurred, bleeding
their outlines, divorced from
the mirror's face.

Behind her, the white satin quilt
hugs the bed like heavy fog,
and the side table with its vase of blue
hyacinths is breathlessly in focus,

but the wives in the mirror merge
and split, mouth words with their eyelashes,
dance rumba with their elbows, sexy
burlesque with their knees, stretch
then shrink. They make the eyes dizzy
like a bad carnival ride.

She takes off the glasses, wipes
her lids, and wonders if the butterfly
who grew vulture wings was just a man
mad with rippled eyes.

This Is How We Love

What they say is true—
you *can* inhale it like a vapor ghost,

like a secret kiss in a hotel bathroom,
a tongue catching light like rain.

Tango

She stays in bed, hangs curtains
over her face, tassels
on her tongue, presses
fists over her belly.

The rocket at the base
of her spine is out of fuel,
valium tap-dances on those lids,
serenades her heart.

In the plastic half-light of the room
a pair of shoes trembles by the door.
Maybe, she thinks.

But this dance *is* tango,
the floor graveled with uneven stones,
the dips are precarious,
the men don't always catch.

1

You know you are in trouble when
you ache at the base of the stomach.
You know you are done for
when he looks away and the rope
tugs like a boat moored to the quay.

But this is LA and love is like a warm day.
So he puts on his leather shoes,
she, her red high heels, and they walk
past Hollywood toward Sunset.

Tenth Anniversary

She picks up a knife, disassembles herself
piece by piece until she's a grisly mound.

The cleaning woman sweeps her under the couch,
the dog pulls her out, chews on her tongue,
the children play ball with her heart,
the husband snorts, throws up his hands,
splits open the back of her head to have a look.

Fault Lines

She keeps losing things—
her wedding band, for example.

Can't go home because her keys
were seized by armed question marks,
can't sleep because her dreams
were abducted by an always-leaving God.

She goes searching for her voice
inside a gun's throat, in a vulture's nest,
between the folds of her sex; finds it
in the fault lines of a cracked mirror.

#2

Winter sunlight falls,
shatters on her doorstep.

The porch paint has peeled,
sad brittle pieces like fragments
of a broken heart.

How a cloudless day full
of promises closes.

Everything is fiction except
for what hides in the heart.

Freedom

In the garden's thinning air
the fish are dying in the pond.

Have you ever felt a thousand jellyfish
staring with eyes that are not eyes?

She folds and unfolds her roadmap.
Everything possible is also impossible.

#3

Where are you now?
You sound giddy. Have you
been drinking? What's that noise
in the background?
Is there someone with you?

I love you more
than all the turnips and tulips.
I love you more than all raindrops.
I love you beyond what is beyond.
I ache for you. You have no idea. No idea.

What Slides inside the Throat

There are words that give cavities,
secrets that bring on cramps,
lies that can poison an entire clan.

Betrayal is a room without a window,
it's a swollen heart that smells of decay.

To blunt the knife edge of her thoughts,
she listens to dead tenors' arias—those
scratchy recordings of masculinity—
waltzes with muscular ghosts among her dying
garden's white oleander trees.

How he had once said I love you, and how
she had swallowed this untruth like vodka.

Illusion

Un-whole isn't the same as un-holy,
isn't the same as dead.

In the valley, apples cling tenaciously
to leafless arms.

She presses her spine against a breeze,
mistaking it for a wall.

#4

I'm an atheist, he says, *but now*
I'm thinking maybe there is a God,
maybe you are like the sea
Moses parted—

and he knocks open her legs, pauses,
scratches his chin, says, *but,*
there was a drought and the sea
was perhaps a shallow lake
the Israelites waded through.

Maybe you are like the moon
Mohammad split in half like a heart,
he says, unbuttoning her red blouse,
but how can a rock that orbits
this earth be so neatly be carved?

She stares at his naked chest, imagines
kneeling among tall kowtowing waves
like a centerfold Cleopatra shaking off
water from her long wavy hair; or standing

in thin silver silk on a moon that's been
split and now hangs like two breasts
pressed against the dark body of a man—
a black man with more muscles and faith,
fewer words and no pauses in making love.

Divorce

It's snowing inside
and the house is shocked
by the children's absence,
the wide-eyed Barbie,
the deflated basketball.

Ask Her Any Question and She Will Answer Like Glass

Or maybe it isn't that simple.

At first she wants it. Wants it
so hard she throws away everything.
Wakes up alone inside
a skin tattooed by living.

Now she stands by a black river.
She will wash her sex in this ink,
let the fish eat her desire.

This is how she gives her soul a bath.
It's better than time travel to set things right.

#5

They are drinking scotch on Sunset Blvd.,
a block from the Scientology church,
the tourist trinket shops, and the sex parlors.

She tells him she's an alien, lifts her arm to show her scar,
the way she flashes her passport at immigration.

He bends across the narrow table, pushing aside plates,
squints, then runs a finger along the carved hairline
and whispers, *yes, yes.*

The Hallway

A man in a bright blue t-shirt and
red shoes cries on the phone.
A child runs the corridor while his
older brother fidgets like an injured bird.

Shoes glued to the floor, palms heavy
on her lap, it's like waiting in a sweat puddle
outside the school principal's office.

Her husband sits on a bench across, taps
his feet, fixes his eyes on the man, the child,
the older boy, anything but her: the poem
he kept in his breast pocket for twenty years.

The lawyers come.
The courtroom jaws unhinge.

The Art of . . .

She soared to the moon on the back
of a pink seagull, ate cheese puffs
with her mustached father in a balloon
high above Mars, or licked saffron
ice cream in a field of lollipops
grown by a band of whirling dwarfs.

The children gathered daily
for their dose of tall tales, believed,
as if she, with her wild hair, licorice black
eyes, and snowball cheekbones,
were the daughter of a poet and a witch.

In high school she rolled her stories
like weed between math sheets,
in toilet paper, yellow school bulletins;
smoked and sold, gifted and inhaled.

Addiction to telling melted truth doesn't
land a girl in rehab, but it does make
a red rhymer out of one, a woman who sighs

I love you to the one who pulls her
into a hot tub of glass and painted tiles;
a man who guitar-plays her inner thighs
and dances tattoos of flying insects
across his wide, muscle-hilled arms.

Help Her Leave

Pack the *Wasteland,* Shakespeare, and Lord Byron,
leave the *Da Vinci Code,* stacks of holy books.

Fold the Persian rugs, unhook the crystal lamp,
pull from under the bed the children's dirty socks.

Stow the stuffed bear, the monkey, the blue-veined doll;
pack the toy trains, the basketball, the Lego trucks.

Sweep the kitchen clean of crumbs,
wipe the tiny hand marks from the glass tabletops.

Don't look out the window with its twenty-year view,
don't talk to the roses, the citrus trees, the bougainvilleas.

Open the front door, release the butterflies.
The cat stays buried by the willow, beneath painted rocks.

#6

Two electricians argue in Russian
over how to run a line from a chandelier
to the dimming switch.

The one with long eyelashes asks
if he can play his CD on her stereo.

Argentine Tango, he says,
after the chandelier is hung,
the dimming switch tested.
You like?

She says, *I like*, and he offers
to teach the steps, puts his hand
on the small of her back, plants his eyes
on her breasts, braless beneath this flimsy
red blouse, tilts her steep until her curls
river the checkered tiles.

That night, she puts on a blue strapless gown,
invites in her dead lover's emaciated ghost.
He comes in through the window, takes her
in his bony moonbeam arms, and they tango
like two broken violins in love.

The Secret Code

This is how a woman unfolds sin by sin,
wipes away the memories
that condense like fog
on the glass of her heart,
as if what's beneath
deciphers life.

When she thinks of home, it is always in the colors of night.

Tomorrow is just a name
meaning: another day, another
story hung from a string thin as an eyelash.

Fat ghosts hover above the bed where she worshipped a silver
wolf.

The better to see you my dear,
the better to feel your skin,
soft as powdered
gold.

Yet,
when she thinks of her husband,
it is sometimes with softness.

Sanctuary

Home is a missing tooth.
The tongue reaches
for hardness
but falls
into absence.

"Where is the life
we have lost in living?"

—T. S. Eliot

The House on Stilt Legs

I have just arrived, and the air is wet.
The breeze lifts up my skirt
to have a look.

The neighbors file in, bring
baked plantains, chickpea roti,
goat curry so spicy my eyes melt.

They finger my curls, touch
my long black eyelashes.
Laugh.

In the street, boys hiss
at my back with lips, tongue,
and breath. Young men

emerge skinny and dark,
from among tall sugar cane
fields, machetes in hand.

Just for you, they say, and pull out
long, clean, fat stalks, bleeding
sugar from the cut.

The four-leaf clover holes that line
the edges below my bedroom ceiling
are portholes to the stars.

Fireflies come in with the breeze,
turn my mosquito net into a green-
flashing southern sky. I tell them

about Tehran's dusty streets and high
walls, gardens where every tree steals
innocence from eyes, where every rose

offers her thorns to stitch mouths,
where crows blacken the sky snitching
on the comings and goings of the moon.

I sketch in the air the bell jar
in which I lived and almost died,
show them the roof of my mouth

where a secret grows like moss, the inside
of my belly button where the cord to my
homeland's womb remains uncut.

Lost in Trinidad

Sexless and pale, Mother Superior and her side-kick, Sister
Anne, watch me. They say, *How do you do,* in clench-mouthed
British beat, then shepherd me into the school's makeshift
chapel, kneel me before a cross and a large framed poster of
Madonna and Child.

Immaculate Mary,
Your praises we sing;
You reign now in splendor
with Jesus our King.

Sister Anne bends over my small form, eyes big as
the apocalypse, and whispers: *This is where we eat the body*
of our Lord, drink his sacred blood. She makes me sit on a red-painted
cement bench in the yard, hands me a list of English B verbs
to memorize: Behaving, Blending, Belonging . . .

My schoolmates gape at my legs, white as *frosting*
on a bridal cake, trace their fingers along my collarbone,
bumpy cheeks, and thick brown eyebrows.
I feel like a Persian kebab stick in ugly uniform.

The Indian girls won't oil my hair—too curly, they say.
The black girls refuse to braid them—not kinky enough.

But the music teacher shows me his teeth, says he will
teach me English through songs. In the deserted schoolyard,
he sits beside me and sings.

Yellow bird,
Up high in banana tree
Yellow bird
You sit all alone like me

When he strums his guitar, his sixth finger wiggles like a fat dangling worm.

Buried Stories

Mother says bury
your shaming stories
deep in your liver,
take them with you
to your grave.

But a burdened liver
explodes in the pressed
quiet of the earth, poisons

the worms, the water,
the soil, the crops that push
toward the sun, that feed our children.

Pickles and Donuts

Cold basements remind me of the dead
fruit my mother smothered in sugar, the phallic
pickles souring in tight-lipped jars.

I keep my school uniform stained, my
long hair pulled back tight, my walnut
breasts cloaked with baggy shawls,

tell my friend next door, about the red
jam donut beneath our skirts, teach her
the waist-twisting dance of wrapping childhood's
curtain around her body so soon unfolded
like voodoo air from an uncapped perfume bottle.

I breathe in books that turn my eyelashes
to blue feathers, my eyelid's veins into delicate
wing-bones that flap and lift, travel me
to an island house on stilt legs.

She eats the stone pages of an old Quran,
comes of age at dusk where bombs fall
on paved roads and the sky rains scalding
lava that streams and streams, carries her
to the sharp edge of the world.

The Prince

The night of the dance I wore
an ankle-length caftan, hiding
my body beneath its airy flow, flat
shoes not to be too tall,
and my roommate's lipstick,
brighter than orange juice.

He was a prince who could have picked
any of the boarding-school girls—
Suzie with one eye blue,
full-breasted Victoria,
or the girl from India with a waist
slender as a drumstick tree.

But the sixteen-year-old Saudi royal
asked *me* for the first dance, then the second,
then for the rest of the night, as boys and girls
disappeared into dark corners while
chaperones dozed off in the hall
nipping Hennessy from tiny silver flasks.

My prince was shy, but not too shy
to slowly drop his hand and squeeze,
his lips on mine, the knife
in his pocket on my groin.

On the ride back the girls taunted me,
Camel driver's virgin, imitated my accent

singing, *Don't touch the merchandise,*
mocked me for pushing away the fetching prince
so hard he fell on his ass and twisted his wrist.
What did he do? Stick his finger up your . . . ?

That night I packed my bag, slipped out
just as the sun exhaled its first breath into night,
took the first Eastbourne rail to London.
I hid beneath a beat-up hat, collar pulled up,
and by the time the headmaster was informed,
called the police and my anxious parents overseas,
I was at my clueless cousin's boarding house nibbling
baklava, drinking hot tea from a chipped cup.

I shivered beside a coin-operated heater, ate
fish and chips on yesterday's newspaper, and read
Neruda, Farrokhzad, for a week, Tolstoy, and Austen.
Quietly I thanked my father for giving me time
to strengthen the sinew that held my heart.

It rained and I didn't go out, avoided my big-boned
cousin with her roto-rooter tongue and the nose
of our grandmother who could smell anything
rotting inside the heart. I turned the cracked mirror
in my room towards the wall. Someone
had scribbled "HELP" on the back.

The rose-splattered wallpaper looked scrubbed
with day-old coffee. The lone sofa sagged
with the weight of absent occupants the way
my lips still felt the heaviness of that first kiss.

In the end what mattered, I learned,
were the smallest blessings:
the milk-sweetened tea or the miracle
of scalding water from the ancient bathtub faucet.
What counted were my widowed cousin
holding her own in a foreign land,
and the grit to say no
to what is hurled—words, glances, bullets, all.

Best Friend

She is violent with her skin.
Her white cotton gown smells
as she sickens, soaks the bloodstain
in tears and cold bathhouse water,
washes what pressed against her
newly sprouted breasts,

the manicured hands
that pinned hers to the damp
soil, the eyes so close to her own
when he entered, pumped
like a vulgar dog, finished
like a deflating ball.

For this,
her body still,
soul numb-cold as a river,
forever keeps on
moving away.

The Rosetta Stone

Sakineh is a popular name.
Means quietude.
Also, feminine.

Saket 'o Samet is a compliment
paid to young women,
scoring them marriage points.
Meaning: silent and mute.

Saleeteh is an insult reserved only for women.
Means: one who bothers men; a shrew.

Bakereh is a girl with an "unstained skirt,"
a "Miss" as in a girl not yet married.
A female virgin.

And *Bakereh-shenasi* is a specialty.
Means parthenology, a word not found
in most English dictionaries.

At Journey's End Resort

I pay to float among
white-bellied whale sharks,

but when circled by a group,
five pairs of gills on twenty-foot bodies,

three hundred tiny teeth
in each capacious mouth,

I bolt back into the boat shivering
from a raw sense of end.

That night I swim in cold dreams
among those sharks, give them

my lines and limbs as if in repentance
for sins I cannot undo, give

until nothing remains but fear-rippled
water—salty, metallic, and pink.

And when the next morning I tuck
my rebel curls under a fedora, I suddenly

remember the sharks had also wanted
my hair, but I had kept it back.

In the mirror I spy a shadow on the fedora's
rim, pull back the front flap and there, poised

inches from my eyes, a large black scorpion
stares back with just as much surprise.

In one move my hat is a flying saucer,
twirling through the bathroom air, landing

with a plop on the cool blue tiles,
trapping the clawed creature underneath.

A uniformed man is summoned. He comes
with a brown rod, a net, asks: should the scorpion live?

I decree death for the creature
who had not struck. That night, I drink

down a bottle of rum, refill it with bitter regret
and resolve to give the sharks my hair.

Dream Labyrinth

My house grows doors
that open to mahogany-
paneled rooms,
to a kitchen
with fifty copper pots,
and a stove wide as a swimming pool;

And on top of this,
is a pan of uncut noodles,
a creaky door that unlocks, pushes
open to a familiar alley blind
behind a crooked house
with black cherries floating
in its pond; a man reading
darkness like a good book, shouts
his wares from a distance.

I wake up, my hair a spreading pile
of mourning black, crushed . . .

Rearrangement

It isn't smoky in this California bar
but the music is loud and the martinis stiff,
and I'm thinking about the odd
arrangement of the human form.

If only I could skin the world, gut it
under the red lamps of this crowded bar,
hang its insides on the electric wires
between the lampposts outside:

and just before sunrise put it all back
the way I see fit. Skin inside out,
one eye looking straight at the heart.

At the Temple of Bloomingdale

The woman behind the Smashbox counter,
says my face is all wrong;

that I must wear eyeliner thick and black, never
let the lines wander off without meeting;

compliments my bone structure but
calls my coloring "monochromatic"—
brown hair, brown eyes, brown eyebrows.
Brown nipples too, I say.

She brushes emerald shadow on my lids,
outlines my eyes with purple, her face so close
to mine, I note how the blue, the brown and the gold
are blended to code on *her* lids, how her eyebrows are
drawn with a pencil, then powdered to stay.

She surveys my pores from beneath a large magnifying
glass, counts my wrinkles, clucks her tongue, asks
if I use a toner, brings out bottles and jars guaranteed
to smooth cracks, fill in the lines. When I leave
I am poor and look like the whore of Babylon.

How Hard Is It to Write a Love Song?

Last night a sparrow flew into my house,
crashed against the skylight and died:
I want to write a love song.

Poppy seed cake on china plate,
tea like auburn gold, the New York Times
open on the table, black with news,
and the man I still love with me.

The newspaper says in Conakry a man is
sticking his Kalashnikov into a woman. Now
he's pulling the trigger.

Hummingbirds zip through the garden.
My lover slowly rocks in the hammock,
a spy novel on his stomach.

I flip a page and a Nigerian soldier
shoots a man because he's parked badly,
and takes the dead man's hat.

The bougainvillea has burst into pinks and reds,
the colors of Kabul's sidewalks after a suicide attack.
The child next door squeals with laughter.

How hard is it to write a love song?
A little in-the-moment swim,
a bit of Bach—perhaps.

Yellow to Blue

I offer every ghost
who comes to my bed
a cigarette,

catalogue every untruth
I've told,
postpone everything
urgent,

hire mourners in case
I jump, water
the wilted flowers on my
bedroom walls.

There is no calm
in patience,
no restlessness
in motion.

You can't assign yellow
to blue,
and adjectives are sick
of being married
to nouns.

I want to go Da-Da-Da,
say *NO*
laced with *yes*,

paint horizons
over horizons,

because I know
a river never stops
stroking itself
towards the sea,

and cigarettes don't
kill what's already
dead.

Quasars

A beautiful woman
giving birth to a child.

You can't divorce the sky
because love is blue.

Or maybe we have it backwards.
It is the air who flutters through birds,
the body that pounds in the heart.

Didn't your grandmother's small
courtyard swing wide to a wooden blue door,
her guests seated and served to thimbles
of steaming sweetened tea?

She says nothing, but opens her lips.

Everything is about away.
The trees past a train, train blurring
houses, the river away from its bed,
a horizon to horizon sun.

Clocks keep dignity, not time.
Journey is a rocky path with many doors.

I am a custodian of memory,
the murderer of saplings.
I leak from my skin.

Because

Because lemonade is a whole lot of sour
masked,
happiness is the added sugar to what is.

Because a lake is whole lot of water in a big
hole,
eyes can become tar pits of sadness.

Because the heart is a pump made of
flesh,
love can be deported to a left foot's little toe.

Because a soul is a poem fleshed with
words,
I must now stop writing about the poem.

"Whenever you find yourself on the side of the majority, it is time to reform."

—Mark Twain

Footnotes of a Sour Savior

Today's news
is wrapped around
tomorrow's dead fish.

Could it be that all windows
open to fiction while reality
burns on our stoves?

Time chimes in gods' bell-towers,
and bottled sunlight gathers dust in caves.

Death is a bearded vagrant pushing a cart
and love is but a shadow,
coreless and crumbling, like purity.

And God? God is always leaving, leaving.

The Circle

What is the miracle of faith?

Rebirth is not an option.

A parrot in the belly of a dolphin
makes as much sense as sin.

The more I stretch,
the shorter I become.

How much for my tongue?
My heels? My knees?

Can a tree unroot?
Shoulders blossom flippers?

I melt the air in my mouth,
dribble it on this circle.
How much for that?

Blank is not white.
White is not without color.

The Green of Iran

No departures here.
In Tehran out and in are closed,
under and over, stained.

Yet how green is the green of her sky.
The clouds bleed this green,
green the river, fields of rice,
the moss that grows
on Alborz mountain rocks.

The earth births this green
that the ants carry through
the cracks of Evin's walls.
The birds shit green
on the turbans of bearded men.

Green is the green of this land,
the poplars lining parks,
green inked letters of lovers
holding hands in dark alleys
where green is the color of eyes,
the smell of dust swept clean.

Green are the ears of geraniums
on windowsills, and feet
of roses in backyards,
and the color of ponds
populated with green-
scaled fish, and frogs who sing
to the night dreams of green.

I Am Neda

Leave the Basiji bullet in my heart,
fall to prayer in my blood,
and hush, father
—I am not dead.

More light than mass,
I flood through you,
breathe with your eyes,
stand in your shoes, on the rooftops,
in the streets, march with you
in the cities and villages of our country
shouting through you, with you.
I am Neda—thunder on your tongue.

On June 20, 2009, Neda Agha-Soltan, a twenty-six-year-old Iranian woman and a student of philosophy who was attending a demonstration in Tehran protesting the vote-count fraud in the reelection of President Mahmoud Ahmadinejad, was shot in the heart by a member of Basij militia. In the jittery cell phone video of a bystander who captured the murder, we hear a man wailing her name, begging her to stay, not to leave, as blood gushes from her chest and streams out of her mouth. The name Neda means "the call" in Persian.

Rajkowska's Palm in the Land of Auschwitz

In a roundabout on Warsaw's Jerusalem Avenue,
a tree's spiny leaves mock the city's dour winter.
It's absurdity at its best, like a boat made of lead,
a road of upright nails, a dove nesting on a swastika.

The tropical specter slows the cold throng,
lifts their eyes to take in the proud lone mirage erupted
from snow—a prayer for a people plucked out.

Perhaps this palm will remind them that the ash-tinged grey
painted across their town belongs to the bed
of an ocean, or inside distant clouds;
that time itself is a passenger inside
a driverless bus, spinning out of control.

"Artist Joanna Rajkowska erected her artificial canary island date palm on the 12th of December 2002, following one and a half year's preparations. Origins of the project date back to the artist's journey to Israel in 2001 and her attempt 'to make people aware' of the significance of Jerusalem Avenue to Warsaw, the street's history and the vacuum caused by the absence of Jewish community. It was supposed to be also a social experiment, testing whether the Polish society is ready to absorb such a culturally alien item. The spot at which the palm has been placed before the year 2002 had been used for a Christmas tree."
—From the tree's official website

The Exiles

Look how the foamy-mouthed sea
licks its own shores,
splashes and rolls
furious in its coming to reclaim
its fish from death's tanks
in crowded cafes.

The sea comes, it comes
but does not arrive . . .

as we never arrive
no matter how intent
we are to liberate our kin
from hungry bearded serpent gods,
window-starved rooms,
from under voice-proof veils.

Our tongues lick time's spiny slates,
bleed saliva flavored with abstractions:
"injustice," "violations," "freedom,"
our eyelashes thrash in indignation,
and our eyes claim pain . . .

but like the sea, we keep coming
fiercely, and never arrive.

We Suckle on Fantasies

It's a starless night in California's
Highway 33 and my headlights
drill through the unnatural darkness.

I turn on the radio, Wagner's
Die Walküre bursts as if on cue
with a strange light that drops
into my view.

I pull over and watch from the window
a bright dot in the sky trail saffron strands
then explode into a bridal veil and disperse.

That night it reappears in my dreams to Vivaldi's
Sabat Mater, a seraph upward-winging into heaven,
swirling until I'm standing on a calyx of light.

The morning papers have its picture in color:

> *A missile, shot from an underground silo*
> *hits targets at a range in the Marshall Islands*

Coming Home

Who sews coffin flags of fallen soldiers?

A roomful of women, fingers bloodied
in grief, in haste?

Or an efficient factory-machine—
one flag per minute?

Keeping Time with Blue Hyacinths

A Nowruz Sonata
in 7 Movements

Prelude

In the pause between spring rain
a woman pirouettes in a field.

Her skin is a thousand mirrors.

1st Movement

A young girl, pigtail tied back
with pink bows wide as her smile,
in a purple dress with puffy sleeves,
new red patent-leather shoes with
shiny straps that crisscross over
white ruffled socks, waits eagerly.

Mother has set the *haft-sin* table for Nowruz.
A goldfish in a crystal bowl; an egg
that will roll when the bull tosses
the world over to its other horn;
and seven tokens starting with *sin*, the Persian *S*:
sabzeh—samanu—senjed—seer—seeb—somāq—serkeh

If children were allowed the word "orgy,"
this is what they would imagine, this
table laden with all-you-can-eat clouds
of scented Yazdi cotton candy, globes
of creampuffs, almond baklava dripping
with buttery syrup, sliced yellow cake so moist
it glistens, saffron cookies that crumble
in watering mouths.

2nd Movement

This year a Simourgh egg sits
on every *haft-sin* table. Large
and golden, it twirls like a planet, mesmerizes
even the bulging eyes of Haji Firuz.

And on the thirteenth day
of the new year, everyone puts the egg
under their pillow to keep it warm.
At night, we take it up to the roof, singing
our rebellion to the moon: *Allahu-Akbar,*
while the Shah's men shoot in the streets.

But when the time comes,
the egg hatches a slathering wolf.

3rd Movement

The goldfish on the *haft-sin* table is as far
from home as my family in exile.

My life whirls:
DC, Baltimore, Chicago, LA, colleges,
love affairs, broken hearts, homes,
disappointments, celebrations.

Twenty, thirty, forty, a hundred . . .
I'm a thousand years old and still
the *seven-sin* table in my mother's house
remains unchanged:
sabzeh—samanu—senjed—seer—seeb—somāq—serkeh

4th Movement

We collect languages, flags, learn
to cook macaroni and cheese, drink coffee,
and replace Googoosh with Madonna,
Gharib Afshar with Jay Leno,
but make no mistake, we never lose

our voice. *Seda, Seda*, said Forugh Farrokhzad,
tanha sedast. Seda keh jazbeh
zare-hayeh jahan khahad shod.
Chera Tavaghof konam?

I channel her voice:

Voice, voice, only voice remains.
Voice seeping into time.
Why should I stop?

5th Movement

In Los Angeles a rock smashes
through the kitchen window, lands
on my mother's *haft-sin* table,
a new S: *Stone.*

In my language the liver is dearer
than the heart, yet
when it is torn, it's the heart that cries.

If we pile our stories high,
maybe we can reach God.

But for now, mother keeps
the jagged rock that came uninvited,
on her table:
sabzeh—samanu—senjed—seer—seeb—somāq—serkeh . . . stone

6th Movement

Look. Now. Here. How I tremble
before this table, a shimmering reflection
in a thousand mirrors on a tall
shapely woman. She pirouettes in baritone green,
soft as Rumi's voice, sacred
like seven songs salvaged from an eighth sin
on a *haft-sin* table.

7th Movement

Everything happens in sevens,
like the movements of this sonata
each a *sama*—meditative pirouettes—
between everything seen and unseen,
stumbling on nothing.

This is how we become pleasure,
a dance, a sin, uncommitted,
grace in movement, movement in grace,
like the lifting of a hand, the back-bending rise
of the chest, the rotation of the heart.

Time passes us just as we each
pass time, and this is how we keep
time with the spring's blue hyacinths,
with the rotation of a goldfish
searching for home.

Notes on "Keeping Time with Blue Hyacinths: A Nowruz Sonata in Seven Movements"

Nowruz: the first day of spring and the beginning of the year in the Iranian calendar.

haft-sin: literally meaning seven-S, the traditional table setting to mark arrival the New Year. It includes seven specific items, all starting with the letter *s, sin* (س) in the Persian alphabet:

sabzeh: wheat, barley, or lentil sprouts, symbolizing rebirth.

samanu: sweet pudding made from wheat germ, symbolizing affluence.

senjed: dried oleaster fruit, symbolizing love.

seer: garlic, symbolizing medicinal cures.

seeb: apples, symbolizing health and beauty.

somāq: sumac, symbolizing sunrise.

serkeh: vinegar, symbolizing old-age and patience.

Simourgh: a large, benevolent bird in Persian mythology that is believed to purify the land and waters and hence bestow fertility.

Haji Firuz: a symbol of the rebirth of the Sumerian god of sacrifice, Domuzi, who was killed at the end of each year and reborn at the beginning of the New Year. On the day of Nowruz, he wears a red costume, paints his face black (an ancient Persian symbol of good luck) and sings and dances in the streets and at private and public gatherings.

Sizdeh Bedar: the thirteenth day after the New Year, a day of festivities marked by spending time outdoors, often accompanied by music and dancing. A literal translation is "expelling bad luck on the thirteenth day of the year."

Forugh Farrokhzad: arguably Iran's most daring and significant female poet of the twentieth century. For more information about her life and poetry refer to *Sin: Selected Poems of Forugh Farrokhzad*, translated by Sholeh Wolpé (University of Arkansas Press, 2007.)

Acknowledgments

These poems have been in making for the past five years. Chris Abani, Tony Barnstone, Elena Karina Byrne, Nathalie Handal, and Suzanne Roberts—I can't thank you enough.

I also wish to express my gratitude to Hamid Saeidi and the Farhang Foundation, who commissioned me to write a meditation on Nowruz, the Persian New Year, for a performance at the Los Angeles County Museum of Art in March 2012. The result of this effort was "Keeping Time with Blue Hyacinths: A Nowruz Sonata in 7 Movements," which closes this book.

Many thanks to the staff and editors of the following publications in which some of the poems in this book, either in their present form or a variation thereof, have appeared:

Guernica Magazine, The Warwick Review, Callaloo, Two Review, Sierra Nevada Review, The Rumpus, Zacola Public Square, The Other Voices International, The Great River Review, The Atlanta Review, Connotation Press, The Forbidden: Poems from Iran and Its Exiles, Monstrous Poems, FrontLine's Tehran Bureau, Voices [Education Project], The Kokanee, and *Love and Pomegranates.*

And as always my immense gratitude goes to my editor, Larry Malley of the University of Arkansas Press, for his foresight, love of literature, and genuine interest in his authors.